Emirates

LEGENDS
LFL
1
LFL

YAMAMOTO
NUTRITION

QATAR
AIRWAYS

MIAMI
HEAT
HEAT
NBA

11
11

Heart
LEGENDS
LFL
7
LFL

RED SOX
TPX

Radio
2

Wilson

molten

City of
Santa Monica

Wilson
NFL

ARGENTINA
5
11
11

2006

ARE
ZOO

TITLE

Made in the USA
Monee, IL
29 November 2024

71664269R00021